Table of Contents

How does access to resources influence people's lives?

Notes

Seattle: Up and Down—and Up Again

by Alexandra Hanson-Harding

1   American cities have gone through many economic changes over the course of history. Some have experienced rapid growth due to new industries and technologies. Others have seen the decline of once-thriving businesses. Most cities, like Seattle, Washington, face economic ups and downs over time.

2   Today, Seattle is famous for its high-tech companies, such as Microsoft and Amazon. But when Seattle was established in the 1850s, its economy was supported by a lumber mill. Lumberjacks cut logs, and the lumber from those logs was shipped to help build a booming San Francisco. This profitable business helped Seattle grow.

3   When the railroads arrived in the 1880s, Seattle's population grew quickly. In the first half of 1889, Seattle gained 1,000 new residents every month. Seattle even rebuilt after a serious fire damaged much of its business district.

During the 1850s, lumber was shipped from Seattle's port to San Francisco to help build the city.

4

Seattle Time Line

This view of modern-day Seattle shows the Space Needle and Mt. Rainier.

1851	Seattle is founded.
1889	Seattle has a great fire but rebuilds.
1897	Klondike Gold Rush makes Seattle rich.
1940s	Seattle-based Boeing Aircraft supplies warplanes for WWII.
1971	Boeing lays off 40,000 workers.
1979	Microsoft moves to Seattle area.
1987	Starbucks opens about 17 stores.
2014	Seattle is booming again.

Notes

4   In the years that followed, Seattle became a "boom or bust" town. In the 1890s, a nationwide depression crippled Seattle's economy. Then, in 1897, the Klondike Gold Rush began. Seattle became the main supplier for the thousands of miners who came to Alaska. Seattle was a "boom" town once again.

5   Like most cities, Seattle went "bust" during the Great Depression of the 1930s. The city recovered when Boeing, a Seattle aircraft company, supplied war planes for the U.S. government during World War II. By the 1970s, however, another economic downturn forced Boeing to lay off more than 40,000 workers.

6   More recently, Boeing has been part of Seattle's growth, along with Microsoft and other high-tech companies that came to Seattle in the 1970s. They were joined by the coffee chain Starbucks in the 1980s. Since that time, many other new businesses have moved to the city. Today, Seattle is up and booming again.

Notes

César:
¡Sí, Se Puede!
Yes, We Can!

Poems by Carmen T. Bernier-Grand

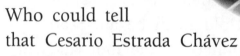

Who Could Tell?

1   *¡Híjole!*
    Who could tell?

    Who could tell
    that Cesario Estrada Chávez
5   the shy American
    wearing a checkered shirt,
    walking with a cane to ease his back
    from the burden of the fields,
    could organize so many people
10 to march for *La Causa*, The Cause?

    Who could tell
    that he with a soft *pan dulce* voice,
    hair the color of mesquite,
    and downcast, Aztec eyes,
15 would have the courage to speak up
    for the *campesinos*
    to get better pay,
    better housing,
    better health?

20 *¡Híjole!*
    Who could tell?

Green Gold

1   *Lechuguero,*
     a lettuce thinner,
     a man, a woman, or a child
     who pulls off smaller plants
5   to make room for bigger plants—
     the *patrón's* green gold.

     Row after row,
     César walked.
     Stooped over, twisted,
10 clawing at the *chuga*
     with *el cortito,*
     a short-handed hoe.

     No boots, just shoes
     sinking in mud,
15 clay clinging to the soles.

     Every day swathed in scarves
     covering his nose and mouth.
     Trying not to breathe,
     trying not to swallow
20 the smelly spray blowing on him.

     Armpits sweating,
     back aching…aching…aching.
     Too tired to feel the hunger.

¡Sí, Se Puede! Yes, We Can!

1   How did César do it?
Asking farm workers to walk out of their jobs.
¡Huelga! Strike!
¡Viva La Causa! Long live The Cause
5   for freedom, dignity, and respect!

How did César do it?
Leading a 300-mile *peregrinación*
of *campesinos*
from Delano to Sacramento.
10   Limping on blistered feet,
the Aztec eagle on their union flag flying.

How did César do it?
Not eating at times
A "Fast for Love"
15   to draw attention to nonviolence.
A "Fast for Life"
to draw the attention of the world
to *campesinos* with breathing difficulties,
campesinos with skin rashes,
20   *campesinos* dying of cancer
because of pesticides
that the government insisted
did no harm.

How did César do it?
25 Asking people to boycott
grapes and lettuce
until the pesticides were banned,
until the *campesinos*
could get better ways to live,
30 ways . . . to live.

Much good came out of it.
"Farm workers are struggling out,
of their poverty and powerlessness."

"¡Sí, se puede! Yes, we can!"
35 *"The answer lies with you and me.*

Yes, We Can!
that the government insisted
did no harm.

César Chávez (1927–1993) was born near Yuma, Arizona, and became a migrant worker at age eleven when his family lost their farm during the Great Depression. After many years as a farm laborer, Chávez started a movement to improve the conditions of workers in the fields of California. He founded the United Farm Workers union and became a champion of civil and human rights. Chávez was described by Senator Robert F. Kennedy as "one of the heroic figures of our time."

Remember to annotate as you read.

Notes

Dolores Huerta

1   Labor leader, community organizer, and champion of farmworkers' rights, Dolores Huerta has devoted her life to improving the lives of those around her.

2   Huerta's father was a miner and farmworker who later became an activist and state politician. Her mother owned a restaurant and hotel in a California migrant worker community. There she provided affordable food and housing for farmworkers' families. Dolores Huerta saw firsthand that employment as a migrant worker meant low pay and little dignity. She understood the difficulties they faced and was determined to help them overcome their powerlessness.

3   In the 1960s, Huerta cofounded the National Farm Workers Association with César Chávez. This organization, now called the United Farm Workers, gave them the voice they needed to fight for equality.

4   Huerta was a great organizer. She helped to organize voter registration drives. She also organized strikes, marches, and boycotts that led to the establishment of a better life for migrant workers. She had the wisdom to use nonviolent methods in all that she did. Her involvement with the workers' movement brought her national attention. Dolores Huerta received numerous awards for her work, including the 2011 Presidential Medal of Freedom. It is the highest honor awarded to a citizen of the United States.

BuildReflectWrite

Build Knowledge

Identify a few key images or details of César Chavez in the poem "¡Si, Se Puede! Yes, We Can!" Based on these images and details, what conclusions can you draw about the kind of person he was?

Details/Images	Conclusions

Reflect

How does access to resources influence people's lives?

Based on this week's texts, write down new ideas and questions you have about the essential question.

_____

_____

_____

_____

_____

_____

Research and Writing

Informative/Explanatory

"Seattle: Up and Down—and Up Again" describes how Seattle was affected by a gold rush in the 1800s. Research another city that was affected by a gold rush, and write an informative report about how the gold rush affected that city.

Choose Your Topic

Conduct a pre-search to identify a city that you would like to research in depth. Construct three or more guiding questions that will help you focus your research on the information you will need to write your essay.

Natural Resources and Workers

by Alexandra Hanson-Harding

1   Throughout the history of the United States, people have often moved to different states for work. Some states are able to create jobs and attract businesses because of their natural resources. People need and use natural resources, such as farmland and oil, so jobs are created and industries grow around those resources.

2   Two states with natural resources that have created jobs and grown industries are California and Texas. Agriculture, or farming, is a major industry that generates around $35 billion a year in California. Businesses that work with these farms also generate billions of dollars. Texas, like California, has a major industry that is based on a natural resource: oil. The oil industry in Texas has created jobs and businesses. Texas ranks in the top ten areas in the production of oil worldwide, so the state needs many workers.

oil workers moving a drill in Texas

a painting of the Mission Santa Clara in the early 1800s

Early Workers in California

3   In the 1700s, Spanish priests came to California to start missions, which functioned as both religious and farming centers. The Spanish introduced many different crops and irrigation systems. As a result, the agricultural industry was born and California's need for farm labor began. Father Junipero Serra founded the first mission in San Diego in 1769.

4   The Spanish priests established farms near their missions where Native Americans were forced to work in the fields under poor conditions. The missions also set up Native American settlements close to their farms so that they could supervise their workers as they also tried to convert them to Christianity. As a result, the Native American culture and way of life was disrupted. Over time, many Native Americans grew angry because of the treatment they received under Spanish rule. They staged several rebellions against the Spanish.

California Farmworkers in the 19th Century

5   In the 1800s, European Americans began moving west to California. Gold was discovered in California in 1848, and in 1849 the rush for gold began. In 1850, California became the thirty-first state in the developing nation. As the population in California grew, so did the need for food. As a result, the agricultural industry continued to grow. Among those who came for gold and then stayed to farm were Chinese immigrants.

6   In the early 1860s, the United States hired Chinese workers to help build the Transcontinental Railroad. When it was completed in 1869, these workers flocked to California. They joined the already-established Chinese farming communities. But in the 1870s, a depression forced European American and Chinese workers to compete for work. By 1882, anti-Chinese prejudice led to the Chinese Exclusion Act. Chinese people could not become U.S. citizens. No more Chinese immigrants could enter the United States. Instead, the United States increased the quotas, or the numbers, of Japanese and Filipino workers who could come to the United States.

California Time Line

1774	Native Americans work on huge mission farms.
1848	Gold is discovered in California.
1869	Chinese come to California for farm work after finishing the Transcontinental Railroad.
1882	U. S. government passes Chinese Exclusion Act.
1880s–1906	Japanese start working on farms; later, Filipinos come, too.
1935	Workers migrate from Oklahoma during Dust Bowl era and take over farm work.
1942	Mexican workers come to the United States on Braceros program.
1964	Braceros program ends.
2014	California faces labor shortages.

This photo shows Japanese Americans at the Manzanar relocation camp.

20th-Century Hardships

7   By 1930, the Great Depression, a period of economic hardship that lasted from 1929 to the early 1940s, forced prices for farm goods to drop. As a result, workers' wages dropped, too. Many European American farmers, fleeing the severe droughts of the Midwest, began searching for jobs in California. These workers moved from farm to farm for work. They were called migrant workers. They struggled to survive because there were too many migrant workers and not enough jobs.

8   In the 1940s, World War II began. During those years, the U.S. government forced California's Japanese Americans into "Relocation Camps" such as Manzanar, deep in California's desert. They were forced into these camps because the United States was at war with Japan and considered Japanese Americans as potential enemies. As a result, many Japanese Americans had their homes and farming businesses taken from them.

Notes

9   During the war, new factory jobs opened up, so many farmworkers left the fields for factory jobs that paid better. But farms still needed workers. The United States started the *Braceros* (manual laborers) program. It gave Mexicans limited visas to work in California's fields, but it prevented them from becoming citizens. The program was controversial because many farm owners broke government rules designed to protect these new farmworkers and instead paid them very low wages. This program ended in 1964, but many "undocumented" farmworkers from Mexico and Central America, who did not have official permission to work in the United States, continued to work in California anyway. By 1965, mostly Mexican and Filipino farmworkers formed unions. These are groups of people who come together to ensure that they receive fair wages and good working conditions from employers.

10   In recent years, California has faced a shortage of farmworkers. Still, few American citizens want to work the state's farms because of the low pay for hard work. So some farm owners rely on undocumented immigrants to harvest their crops. The need for farmworkers, and the debate about legal immigration, is often in the news.

These protesters want undocumented immigrants such as farmworkers to be eligible for U.S. citizenship.

Notes

11   Realizing that agricultural workers are valuable contributors to the state and national economy, California lawmakers are looking for solutions to support agriculture. Some lawmakers say the state should raise farmworkers' wages. Others have suggested allowing undocumented farmworkers the right to become U.S. citizens. The debate continues.

Texas Oil: A Natural Resource

This is what the Spindletop oil rig looked like before it started gushing oil.

12   California is not the only state that has had a complicated history with its resources. On January 10, 1901, Texas was forever changed. An oil well called Spindletop, near Beaumont, Texas, began gushing 100 billion gallons of oil a day.

13   The discovery of oil came along just at the right moment for Texas. Gasoline, a fuel made from oil, had recently been invented. Gasoline was needed for cars, which were becoming popular and affordable to most people. By 1903, Wilbur and Orville Wright used a gasoline engine for the first powered air flight. Ships and trains also used oil for fuel. Oil became a booming state industry.

Texas Oil Workers

14   People who were eager for work flocked to East Texas. Small towns swelled with wildcatters (drillers), roughnecks (new workers), and merchants eager to serve them. They crammed together in boarding houses that charged fortunes in rent, but their wages were high. So most workers were able to pay. Soon many people were making money in different ways from the oil industry.

The University of Texas in Austin, shown here, and many other state universities and colleges in Texas get financial support from oil money.

Oil Taxes Help Texas

15   In a few decades, oil had been found in many different parts of Texas. Tax money from oil revenues helped Texas to build roads, buildings, and even universities. The population grew quickly during that time, but some years were difficult for workers. The Great Depression of the 1930s hit many Texans hard. People could not afford cars, so the demand for oil decreased. Sometimes too many businesses were drilling oil, which led to overproduction and caused oil prices to drop.

Texas Time Line

1901	Spindletop starts oil boom.
1905	Texas starts taxing oil.
1930	Overproduction becomes a problem as more oil fields open.
1960	OPEC becomes competitor with Texas for oil.
1981	Petroleum industry makes up a fourth of state's economy but starts to slip.
1981–2014	Texas diversifies its economy

Oil as a World Commodity

16   During the 1930s, oil was also found in the Middle East in countries like Saudi Arabia. It was even cheaper to produce there than in Texas. In 1960, OPEC, the Organization of Petroleum Exporting Countries, was formed with other countries, including Libya and Venezuela. By this time, Texas no longer set the rules about how much oil would cost. It became just one player in the world market.

17   Since that time, Texas workers have had job opportunities or challenges depending on the price of oil, which continues to go up and down depending on events around the world. To remain a strong competitor, Texas is now using new methods of oil production, such as "hydraulic fracturing," to drill for oil, which has helped to create new jobs for workers.

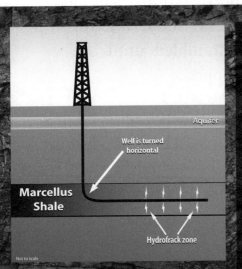

Aquifer

Well is turned horizontal

Marcellus Shale

Hydrofrack zone

Not to scale

Hydraulic Fracturing

Hydraulic fracturing, or fracking, is a new kind of drilling that goes deep beneath the water level under Earth's surface. It breaks up shale rock, releasing oil and natural gas. Some say that it uses too much water and increases the chance of earthquakes. Others say it is helping the U.S. economy, including Texas's oil industry.

Remember to annotate as you read.

Notes

John Henry

1   John Henry's parents knew nothing about agriculture, but they knew how to cultivate a powerful boy. When he was just a baby, he could hoist enormous hammers into the air and hurl them like missiles!

2   When John Henry grew up, he became a steel driver for the railroad. He spent hours hammering spikes into solid rock. It was backbreaking manual labor, and he was unsurpassed. Then one year when the railroad was constructing a tunnel, a salesman showed up and introduced a newly manufactured machine. It was a steam drill. The salesman bragged that it could outwork any man.

3   "It can't outwork mighty John Henry," replied the railroad boss, and so a contest between John Henry and the machine was arranged. The salesman managed to manipulate the newfangled machine into the tunnel. John Henry had only a hammer and two strong arms, but it was his mission to beat the machine.

4   At first, the machine worked faster than John Henry, so John Henry grabbed another hammer and worked with both arms. Without intermission, he hammered. The ground trembled until the machine overheated and stopped.

5   John Henry strode out of the tunnel with his hammers held high in triumph. Then he slumped to the ground. Fellow workers rushed to help him, but it was too late. John Henry had beaten the machine, but he had taken his final breath.

BuildReflectWrite

Build Knowledge

Identify three important events in the history of California, and then describe in a few sentences how these events affected workers.

Events	Effects on Workers

Reflect

How does access to resources influence people's lives?

Based on this week's texts, write down new ideas and questions you have about the essential question.

_____

_____

_____

_____

_____

_____

Research and Writing

Informative/Explanatory

"Seattle: Up and Down—and Up Again" describes how Seattle was affected by a gold rush in the 1800s. Research another city that was affected by a gold rush, and write an informative report about how the gold rush affected that city.

Conduct Research

Use your guiding questions to conduct research this week. Gather information from at least three sources, including both print and online sources. Use your sources to plan your informational report.

Remember to annotate as you read.

Out of the DUST

by Karen Hesse

Notes

Fields of Flashing Light

1   I heard the wind rise,
    and stumbled from my bed,
    down the stairs,
    out the front door,
5   into the yard.
    The night sky kept flashing,
    lightning danced down on its spindly legs.

    I sensed it before I knew it was coming.
    I heard it,
10 smelled it,
    tasted it.
    Dust.

    While Ma and Daddy slept,
    the dust came,
15 tearing up fields where the winter wheat,
    set for harvest in June,
    stood helpless.
    I watched the plants,
    surviving after so much drought and so much
      wind,
20 I watched them fry,
    or
    flatten,
    or blow away,
    like bits of cast-off rags.

25 It wasn't until the dust turned toward the
    house,
like a fired locomotive,
and I fled,
barefoot and breathless, back inside,
it wasn't until the dust
30 hissed against the windows,
until it ratcheted the roof,
that Daddy woke.

He ran into the storm,
his overalls half-hooked over his union suit.
35 "Daddy!" I called. "You can't stop dust."

Ma told me to
cover the beds,
push the scatter rugs against the doors,
dampen the rags around the windows.
40 Wiping dust out of everything,
she made coffee and biscuits,
waiting for Daddy to come in.

Sometime after four,
rubbing low on her back,
45 Ma sank down into a chair at the kitchen
    table
and covered her face.
Daddy didn't come back for hours,
not
until the temperature dropped so low,
50 it brought snow.

Ma and I sighed, grateful,
staring out at the dirty flakes,
but our relief didn't last.
The wind snatched that snow right off the
      fields,
55 leaving behind a sea of dust,
waves and
waves and
waves of
dust,
60 rippling across our yard.

Daddy came in,
he sat across from Ma and blew his nose.
Mud streamed out.
He coughed and spit out
      mud.
65 If he had cried,
his tears would have been mud too,
but he didn't cry.
And neither did Ma.

March 1934

Tested by Dust

1 While we sat
   taking our six-weeks test,
   the wind rose
   and the sand blew
5 right through the cracks in the schoolhouse wall,
   right through the gaps around the window glass,
   and by the time the tests were done,
   each and every one of us
   was coughing pretty good and we all
10 needed a bath.

   I hope we get bonus points
   for testing in a dust storm.

April 1934

Dust and Rain

1   On Sunday,
    winds came,
    bringing a red dust
    like a prairie fire,
5   hot and peppery,
    searing the inside of my nose,
    the whites of my eyes.
    Roaring dust,
    turning the day from sunlight to midnight.

10   And as the dust left,
    rain came.
    Rain that was no blessing.
    It came too hard,
    too fast,
15   and washed the soil away,
    washed the wheat away with it.
    Now
    little remains of Daddy's hard work.
    And the only choice he has
20   is to give up or
    start all over again.

    At the Strong ranch
    they didn't get a single drop.
    So who fared better?

25 Ma looks out the window at her apple trees.
Hard green balls have dropped to the ground.
But there are enough left;
enough
for a small harvest,
30 if we lose no more.

June 1934

This photograph shows a mother and her child who migrated from Oklahoma to California. It was taken by Dorothea Lange, a famous documentary photographer.

SECOND ANNUAL BIRTHDAY BALL
—OF—
PRESIDENT ROOSEVELT
BENEFIT of SUFFERERS of INFANTILE PARALYSIS
AT HIGHLAND PARK CASINO
WEDNESDAY EVE., JANUARY 30, 1935
MUSIC BY TWO ORCHESTRAS
RESERVATIONS 25c COUPLE
CALL 3749-J   LADIES 25c

· ·

The President's Ball

1   All across the land,
    couples dancing,
    arm in arm, hand in hand,
    at the Birthday Ball.

5   My father puts on his best overalls,
    I wear my Sunday dress,
    the one with the white collar,
    and we walk to town
    to the Legion Hall
10 and join the dance. Our feet flying,
    me and my father,
    on the wooden floor whirling
    to Arley Wanderdale and the Black Mesa Boys.

    Till ten,
15 when Arley stands up from the piano,
    to announce we raised thirty-three dollars
    for infantile paralysis,
    a little better than last year.

    And I remember last year,
20 when Ma was alive and we were
    crazy excited about the baby coming.
    And I played at this same party for Franklin D.
    Roosevelt

and Joyce City
and Arley.
25 Tonight, for a little while
in the bright hall folks were almost free,
almost free of dust,
almost free of debt,
almost free of fields of withered wheat.
30 Most of the night I think I smiled.
And twice my father laughed.
Imagine.

January 1935

· ·

The speaker of Out of the Dust, *Billie Jo Kelby, is a young girl who lives in Oklahoma in the 1930s, when the Great Plains of the United States were struck by a devastating drought. The 15,000-square-mile area, which also included Texas and Kansas, was referred to as the Dust Bowl, due to the thick dust clouds and black blizzards that formed when the winds blew loose soil in the air. Crops were destroyed. Hundreds of people died from "dust pneumonia" as a result of inhaling fine particles of dust. Tens of thousands of people left their homes and farms behind, many of them heading to cities and states west.*

Notes

Dust Storm Days

1   Mother stands on the porch and stares at the darkening horizon with despair in her eyes. I quickly become aware of why she is concerned. An enormous black cloud is rolling toward us. It's time to prepare for another dust storm!

2   As the storm approaches, my sister and I scurry around the barnyard rounding up chickens. The gritty air tears at our faces. Once the chickens are in their coop, we dash back to the house. Mother and I carefully arrange wet sheets over the windows to keep out the dust. The sheets provide temporary protection, but soon everything will be covered with grime.

3   By now, the storm has blocked the sunlight, and it is dark outside. Father has been in the barn checking on our mare. When he returns, he is covered with dust and is holding a damp cloth to his mouth so he can breathe.

4   Any damage caused by this dust storm can be repaired, but I'm not sure my family has the forbearance to remain here. Mother swears it's time to move to California, but Father disagrees. He declares that farmers like us aren't welcome in California. It seems unfair, but there's no work for us there. Still, our crops are devastated, and the dust clogs our lungs and wears out our spirit. I wonder—are we strong enough to survive these dust storm days?

BuildReflectWrite

Build Knowledge

What do you think was the author's purpose in writing poems instead of a historical report about people's experiences during the Dust Bowl? What are some of the differences in the two approaches?

Reflect

How does access to resources influence people's lives?

Based on this week's texts, write down new ideas and questions you have about the essential question.

_____

_____

_____

_____

_____

Research and Writing

Informative/Explanatory

"Seattle: Up and Down—and Up Again" describes how Seattle was affected by a gold rush in the 1800s. Research another city that was affected by a gold rush, and write an informative report about how the gold rush affected that city.

Write Your Report

Draft, revise, and edit your informational report using facts, concrete details, quotations, and examples from your sources. Share your report with your peers.

Support for Collaborative Conversation

Discussion Prompts

Express ideas or opinions . . .

When I read _____, it made me think that _____.

Based on the information in _____, my [opinion/idea] is _____.

As I [listened to/read/watched] _____, it occurred to me that _____.

It was important that _____.

Gain the floor . . .

I would like to add a comment. _____.

Excuse me for interrupting but _____.

That made me think of _____.

Build on a peer's idea or opinion . . .

That's an interesting point. It makes me think _____.

If _____, then maybe _____.

[Name] said _____. That could mean that _____.

Express agreement with a peer's idea . . .

I agree that _____ because _____.

I also feel that _____ because _____.

[Name] made the comment that _____, and I think that is important because _____.

Respectfully express disagreement . . .

I understand your point of view that _____, but in my opinion _____ because _____.

That is an interesting idea, but did you consider the fact that _____?

I do not agree that _____. I think that _____ because _____.

Ask a clarifying question . . .

You said _____. Could you explain what you mean by that?

I don't understand how your evidence supports that inference. Can you say more?

I'm not sure I understand. Are you saying that _____?

Clarify for others . . .

When I said _____, what I meant was that _____.

I reached my conclusion because _____.

Group Roles

Discussion director:
Your role is to guide the group's discussion and be sure that everyone has a chance to express his or her ideas.

Notetaker:
Your job is to record the group's ideas and important points of discussion.

Summarizer:
In this role, you will restate the group's comments and conclusions.

Presenter:
Your role is to provide an overview of the group's discussion to the class.

Timekeeper:
You will track the time and help to keep your peers on task.